Fast Horse

☙

MARJORIE SAISER

SANDHILLS PRESS / THE PLAINSWOMAN SERIES
NACOGDOCHES, TEXAS / ORD, NEBRASKA

Any correspondence should be addressed to:

The Editors
Sandhills Press
2274 FM 226
Nacogdoches, TX 75691

sandersmetx@gmail.com

Cover painting is by Janna Harsch.
Book design is by Mark Sanders and Kimberly Verhines.

ISBN 978-0-911015-50-8

Sandhills Press was founded by Mark Sanders at Ord, Nebraska, in 1979. Over the years, the Press has relocated to Missouri, Oklahoma, Idaho, and Texas; the Press, however, has remained rooted to its home state and continues to publish authors from Nebraska and the Plains. Since 1979, Sandhills Press and its subsidiary imprints, the Main-Traveled Roads Chapbook Series, the Plains Poetry Series, and Lewis-Clark Press, have published dozens of authors and books.

The Plainswoman Series is so-named after Kathleene West's book of poems, *Plainswoman: Her First Hundred Years,* which the Press published in 1985 as the first volume in the Plains Poetry Series. The Plainswoman Series honors the late Kathleene West for her contritubitons to Plains poetry and the legacy she created for marginalized women writers of the region forty years ago.

for family

I.
I Don't Know Which River I Am

II.
My Platte River, Mine, I Call It

III.
Crazy New Love

IV.
Homemade Soup and Rolls and Conversation

I.

I Don't Know Which River I Am

I Don't Know Which River I Am

I started out at the confluence
of the Niobrara and the Keya Paha,
where one becomes the other
and the new is neither.
That's me, all my life,
not quite this,
not exactly that.
Tolerance my father had
in abundance;
he could forgive.
That current merged with bitter
because my mother knew
everybody had wronged her.
I'm confluence itself.
I want to be kind,
and I want to be right.
Look out for me--
I'll run you over in the road
but then I'll brake,
get out of my car,
leave the door hanging open,
run back, and hand you the keys.

What Work Was

It was his remedy when he couldn't
make my mother happy,
his fondest wish.
When he went off to war
he figured if he made it back,
things would be perfect. How could they
fail? Beautiful America. He found
that cheaters win
and yet he would not.
Work was his salvation,
red white and blue, long as a
ditch to be dug. It never let up.
Listen, work, thank you, and will you
help me, too? And don't go
thinking he never had fun. He took his
kids to the rodeos: the 2:00 pm
and the 8:00 pm, on the Fourth of July.
He said he'd keep buying
my sister however many hot dogs
until she had her fill. Don't go thinking
I knew what I had. I didn't. But now I
begin to. He said his vote didn't count.
He said he was okay
anyway. There's more
important things than the Almighty
Dollar. He was framing up a house
when he said that, pounding a nail
deep into a two-by-four.
He hit it, square, again and again.

How'd She Win the Heart of That Guy?

How'd she keep his affection,
the one who wouldn't quit
even when she became barbed wire,
even when she shoved.
It's hard to love the unhappy.
A traveling pony show gave her a dog,
one that wouldn't perform reliably.
She took the dog in, though it snapped at her
most of the first day. She squatted down
from time to time with a little ball of raw
hamburger, reached her skinny arm
under the table where Skipper--
maybe she named him or it was a carryover--
had fled to make his stand against the world.
That's how I see her, minus her
unhappiness. I admit it's unfair to
hold unhappiness against her, a double
punishment. Soon she'll be in my top tier;
she's already rising those nights
when I remember her defense of me
after I'm done thinking of her powerful disgust.
There's only the ceiling, only
the same old music, same old CD
over and over to fill the hours because
I, too, do not know which way to run
from emptiness. I love her most
thinking of that ruined show dog,
that snarling white Spitz. She kept her fingers
out of reach of his canines until he was
ready to join with her. I'm ready to join with her.

At the Fair

In the glitz and commerce of the fair
she tried to be good company,
like any girlfriend of her era,
and mostly succeeded, followed my father
around, saw what he looked at.
She didn't have to fake it
at the draft horse competition,
enthusiasm for the way a Percheron can
move, reach forward,
arched neck, flared nostril, a ton of grace.
An animal kept indoors,
small stall, wooden walls to doze against,
but then on command, for the judge,
—run—
float for a moment, haunch and hoof,
over the manicured dust of the arena,
over the captive life.

She Was a Square Peg

She liked to do what the recipe didn't call for.
She liked to add extra raisins to the cake,
serve up a slice for me on a paper napkin,
black coffee, help yourself.
I gave her gifts (I could have done better),
the gift of attention, never a hanky
with MOTHER embroidered in pink
in the scalloped corner.
I know for a fact she liked to solve for X.
She liked to calculate the angle for sawing rafters,
she liked miter boxes, she liked to figure board feet.
Maybe she dreamed buildings,
dreamed of cutting openings in walls,
lifting windows into spaces prepared for them,
their panes flashing as they settled into place.
Maybe they fit perfectly.

Never Any Lotion

Her hands were bigger rather than delicate,
thumbnail flat as a nickel. They could have

passed for men's hands. She liked to work
alongside my father, doing a remodel,

putting up dry wall. She smoothed
the joint compound with a trowel,

sanded the seams, sanded again,
she knew how to work. She took a break,

sat on an overturned empty 10-gallon pail
with her cup of coffee. She didn't add

cream or sugar, didn't smile unless someone
else did, or unless someone was being really

stupid, then a little flash of humor played
around her upper lip until she raised her cup,
took a sip, and got hold of herself.

She Sliced the Potatoes

She stirred them as they fried
in the cast iron skillet, added

small bits of onion. Fragrance and sizzle.
Ease and abundance. She shook salt over,

carried the bowl to the yellow Formica table
where we waited.

I ate the potatoes beside my father.
He had washed at the basin,

his hair still damp. Supper after a long day's
work in the sun. It was possibly holy,

and I had no idea. Isn't it marvelous,
the way things are? The cold milk pouring

into the glass, her hand above it.
The food, the mother, the father.

I moved through the days
easy as air stirring blades of grass,

easy as wind through the field
in which the house lay.

We Took Off in the Ford

My father knew of a store on the highway
where they sold good bologna
so we stopped there—what is better
than a working man on vacation?

It was better than it should be,
all of it: the gray road,
grasslands rolling by the windows,
buckskin horses at a fence,

the gleam of my young mother's hand
as she cut the bologna with a jack-knife,
the tips of her fingers placing a circle of meat
on the cracker, placing a crumble of cheese,

a woman laughing, a man in love, driving,
his mouth open to receive the wafer from her hand.

This is Her Territory, Not Mine

I return to my mother's childhood,
the farm, the house she didn't talk about.

From the windows of the second story
she might have seen me, her future

standing in the yard in mittens and a coat.
And I, looking up, might have seen her

behind the white curtain
where she paused.

Someone had sent her
upstairs to the unheated room

to fetch carrots from
the sand-filled crocks along the walls.

She stands at the window,
her small hand

moving the curtain aside
to look down at me in the yard, waiting.

Unplanned gesture,
then back to her errand. Digging

into cold sand for what is stored there,
the root crop, her unadorned life.

Will You Write About the Painted Ladies?

A cloud of butterflies flew up
in front of her car on the highway
through the sandhills,
and she stopped.

I like to think of her pulling her car over
in the middle of nowhere and getting out
to stand among butterflies,
orange and black filigree wings,
their soundless hinges opening and closing,

some settling on her shoulders, weightless,
their delicate feet in her hair
or along the skin of her outstretched arms.
I think of her saying *I'll never forget this*
I'll never forget this

and asking me to write their colors,
asking me to write to
keep them, thousands and thousands
around her body for a moment,
and years and years on the page.

Hungry for Touch

Asked me to touch her feet, see how
cold they were, she sitting up
in bed, wanting my

hands on her toes, bald nubs,
the nails removed years ago
because of the fungus, so I felt them,

gave them a squeeze,
patted her instep, cold as
I imagine a marble statue, and I left

my hands there like a treatment,
a heat pack from the daughter who had
much going on, buying, selling, progress,

but had made the trip, driven up to
park at her house on a summer day,
the pear tree in her front yard

dangling its small hard fruit
for any bird to peck, and the garage
peeling its paint, shedding as usual.

She had met me at the door, swung it
open and stood with her arms out (never

quite that before), she wearing two sweaters,
and I in my sleeveless guilt.

Fruit to Last

She slices apples into thin half-moons,
arranges rows on a flat pan

which she slides into the oven.
They dry to a brown leather. She tries

to convince me:
they will be tasty this winter.

Pears she instructs me to wrap in newspaper,
each pear enclosed

in a swirl, a drape, a shroud,
and layered into a basket.

Store them, she says,
in the cellar

and I do,
but not all.

This one,
cool round weight in the palm,

this one I redeem,
I bring into the afterlife,

its blossom on the twig
riding the north wind,

the rain it drank,
the morning light it lived in.

Incisors through the yellow skin,
white meat, dripping, into my mouth,

on my lips and chin,
the juices.

Almost Apology

The wind tonight
tears at the tree, which is
heavy with fruit. Mother,

it will crack--stop
pushing further than
wood can stand.

My hair streams out long before me,
now back behind me, now
ruffles into my face. What anger

you had and could not act. Hair
beaten down on the skull,
foolish girl, bad, shameful child.

The wind whips, changes, grabs me,
would, if it had arms,
hold me against its old thin ribs.

Retina

My life moves on the retina
upside down.

If I were anywhere
instead of here on the driveway,
running once more away from home—

if I were at the river,
cranes would land
in the small theater of the retina,

flap in the near dark,
and find a place to settle.
But here is the image of my mother,

inverted, diminished,
windows of her house behind her,
her shoulders round,

arms hanging,
mouth awry,
cheeks wet.

What will I make of this,
of anything?
The fine black lines

of the feet of the cranes
dance upside down
in the globe of the eye.

She recedes, student of broken things.
For me: the windshield and the dash,
my oncoming implacable road.

And So in the Dream

Don't you hate it when
people tell you a dream?
Like you're supposed to care?
And so in the dream I owned this
marvelous old black car
like a Model T,
but the chrome was much heavier
and it was a convertible—like me—
I can be this, I can be that.
And then in the tandem dream—
I always dream two at a time: the left side
has one and the right has its own—
in that dream I was talking to my friend Shell
but I knew Mom was listening. Mom, if you're
listening, I said to the silence
of the kitchen. I said to the flat ears
of the maple cabinet doors, Mom
if you're listening, I said, and it was
the saddest thing.
If you're listening I'm not
crying anymore.
It was a sad thing and happy
at the same time.

Different from Birds that Fly in Daylight

I watched for the nighthawk

in a certain tree, saw where she
liked to rest during the day,

her colors the same
as the limb she chose.

I got used to finding her outline,
took my walk, went back

to fix a meal, soup and crackers
for my mother, one of her last.

My father had been the cardinal, red flash
in the window, a sign,

industrious, clicking, but my mother
tried to be unseen, tried to forgive.

Tonight she circles and dives.
In darkness she works, she wheels.

II

My Platte River, Mine, I Call It

My Platte River, Mine I Call It

The Platte pushes its banks outward,
shoulders the trees to either side,
makes the bed wide,
carries trash from upstream,
bits of foam, plastic cups,
holds a log, floats it,

turns it face up, face down,
keeps going, relentless,
doesn't stop for sunrise
or the weight and noise
of the train along its flank.
The river does not care for

opinions, caresses the sand bars,
puts its arms around,
loves them with gray water
and brown water, covers them
with its own soft body.

If Life Is a Fast Horse, Well Shod

Maybe I join in the talk,
tell my story without straying
too far from the tune. Maybe I've
found the cotton shirt that works
and ordered it in five colors.
Maybe I use certain wine glasses
because they sound good
when they touch one another.
I let the unfair remark
fall to the floor, light-
weight chaff. Maybe I've
decided to surprise myself,
get on the horse again,
crouching low,
fingers clutching the mane,
eyes stinging in cold wind,
the animal beneath me stretching out.
I can almost see the road ahead.
There's a turn coming up.
All I have to do is hang on, hang on.

I Take in the Fox

She is a small shape
under the streetlight. She's stopped
in the middle of Eldon Drive
to have a look at me.
We have one another
for a long moment. I feel
a twinge—maybe fear?—
in my torso, my unsteady legs.
I crave these encounters, these brushes.
Everything silent: the houses,
the full moon with its court of clouds.
Come winter, perhaps I will be glad
to have stored such things.
When the world is dim,
I may want to recall how
the fox paused in the night.
I went to stand in the street
where she had stood,
turned to look at the spot
where I'd been.
Here am I. Here are you.
Even the dark is full of possibility.
Even the visible, while we
stare at it with such purpose,
melts away.

Survived by Talking to Myself

I survived by floating a bit above,
listening to what I was saying
as if it came from another.
Survived the words which hurt,
separated them from my body,
kept them sharp but distant
as a knife. I wrote them down as I had been
taught--nobody taught me, I taught myself.
Survived because I didn't quit kicking, didn't give in
to sinking, though I gave in to crying, which isn't the
same at all. Survived because I said to myself just
often enough that I was good enough,
said it in my head when I couldn't
say it in the room, survived because
I told myself I come from women who
get up every day and go to work
and cook the food even if the baby
has the colic and has to be carried on the hip.
Survived because my father was honest and quiet
and honorable; he couldn't shoot the dog
even when it became necessary, couldn't
aim at the head of the dog that looked to him,
couldn't aim at the chest of the dog while it
breathed. He asked Lyle to do it. Lyle would
later brag. That's Lyle. That's not me.
Because my father could do everything that
needed to be done but couldn't do that,
I will survive.

Girl in the Stucco House

Maybe I can outlive
the sad girl in the stucco house.
I intend to get as close
as a girl from sadness can

to that red star which hung
south of town on summer nights.
It's a long trek, a narrow path I fall
from often but I'm getting up

this morning as my old teacher
taught me and I'm heading off
my newest resentment stuffed inside
my backpack along with my self-

inflicted leg irons. My feet are healed
a little, the common idiom like
manna in my mouth, my one good
eye trained on distance.

Poverty Gave Me Cedar Needles in the Yard

Poverty gave the small house, big enough
to me then, and big enough the pancake
my grandmother laid on my plate,
its edge crisp from the skillet.
Poverty, that giver of gifts, gave
dried leaves on the ground in the grove
while I told myself stories, sagas,
epics on TV, explorers in the wilderness.
Poverty gave the hunger for
school. I hung around the building
in summer, looked in the windows,
ravenous for the classroom and the teacher
who brought the math, that marvel, and
stories in the blue book, words
she chalked for us, for me,
to stoke the hunger. I feel it still
under my ribs, gnawing,
long years after. Thank you, small town
on the rolling grasslands,
for the feast: pot roast and potatoes
and everlasting onions, plenty of gravy
served up time after time
in the house at the end of the road.

Someone Inherited Your Hammer

It hangs on their pegboard, or not;
wish I had it, though I'd only
lift it once in a while, notice its heft,
put it down with a softness.
Every roof you walked on and
repaired. Your boots needing
traction on the shingles while you
figured out what the job needed.
What the job needed was work,
a long day of it, and a lunchbreak when you
came down the ladder for the cooler you'd
packed. Egg sandwiches maybe.
Jar of tea for sure.
I think of you more than ever.
Each day wears on and the dusk arrives.
Color near the horizon deepens,
all the labor of the day behind it,
fading the ordinary out of it,
silhouette arriving:
roof line and chimney and elm tree.
Cool faint aroma of grass rising,
all things giving over to darkness.
What is missing: the sound of your truck,
the starter, the engine, the gravel.
Your eyes as you drive the road home.

Dancing on My Mother's Rug

Dance on the red rug my
father bought her; she would never
say she wanted but she

wanted. And besides,
hadn't the salesman
unfurled rug upon rug

and wouldn't he soon roll them up again?
Buy now Buy now this deal won't last.
I dance as if I had a center, my hair

swinging, body twirling.
I see walls and framed pictures
sliding by, stones of the fireplace

they built together, her hands
holding the stones into place
while he chucked mortar

around them. The sticks of her fingers
wiped the excess away
and everything stayed: stars and planets

in chosen alignment—now
they slip out of place. I dance because
I am bored and because I have feet,

nearly have momentum whirl almost fast enough
my head back with the speed of it
ready so ready Break away Break away.

Still Time, Still Time to Change

> *Still time.*
> *Still time to change.*
> —Mark Doty

On any night the tree can
transform, change

density into filigree
against the moon. The monarch

makes ready in the shell; the case
will split.

And I,
casting, writhing

in my too-small chamber,
don't I have new silks

somewhere? an opening
along a fault in the skin?

The crack, the break, this eternal
reaching toward the new.

III

Crazy New Love

Crazy New Love

When it snowed ten inches,
the business closed at noon

and sent me home.
You were there already,

your car hub-deep in the driveway.
You and I, my house, a blizzard,

remember that? Warmth. Our lair,
a pot of chili. Wind swirling drifts

around the boundaries. Felt
guilty, not a bit,

blankets, chocolate,
the universe filling, perfecting

while snowplows, those small enemy
machines, went blindly up and down

a lattice of lines,
trying to get things back to normal.

Watching You Buy Bread

Tonight in the bakery,
you point to a loaf in the case
as I watch from the car,
the scene like a painting,
as if an artist had good luck
with the color of the crusts,
with the shape of your shoulders,
the collar of your jacket,

the painting having so much light as to
make it dark and splendid here in the car,
the heater running like a soft song.
I roll down the window to join
warm and cold together.
How could I not have seen
how the bare-handed trees hold the fog?

We Take Richie to the Park for a Picnic

The hottest day of summer
you promised Richie
pizza for a picnic.

Finding the perfect table you
high-centered his wheelchair
only twice on the way out
twice on the way back,

and, yes, he was pleased to hold
the pizza box on his knees,
his spotless tennis shoes
banging the metal footrests
At least we did remember his hat
and he made happy noises
when I cut his pizza into cubes.

He laughed at his own joke
when you said it was hot
and he said Wait til tomorrow
or whatever he said. He seemed to
think you could figure it out.

He did love going backwards up over
the more impassable places.
And double-time over the wood chips,
that was good.

I agree with Richie;
I think you are wonderful.
With any luck at all
his sunburn will be minor and
he won't get heat stroke until after
we get another snapshot for his album:
you beside him, his eyes proud,
a dab of tomato sauce on his chin.

Horses, Galloping

We are horses galloping together,
moving shoulder to shoulder, flank to flank.

We are dogs, our tongues dripping;
hot breath of one in the other's mouth.

Outside the room the hiss of tires on the street:
rooster crowing on a dark island.

In the beginning perhaps everything was one,
but creation broke it, a plate falling on stone.

The morning is mine,
all pieces of it.

My knees draw up,
my feet swim to one another in the bed,

flexing, palming, dealing in comfort.
Long slow curve of the rooster's crow.

On the Road, So to Speak

You wanted to go to Luigi's
because, as you said, you were pulling
down good money, you got paid every
Friday, and every Friday you liked to eat.
In the side mirror I saw half my face:
my earring, my uncareful hair. I liked it,
stretched my legs in black stockings
straight out in front of me, like my life.
I liked that car—you let me drive it:
Take my car, you said. So I eased it
down into the farmstead of my ex-in-laws
to pick up my son. Big day, big muscle, big
hood like the bow of a ship. I
braked at the fence, got out, and
waved to the house, the porch, the
disdain. I'm going to indulge for a moment
right here right now before I get back to
working on myself. Because, as the trucker
in the Consolidated Freightways said to me on
the CB after I blew past him in that marvel of a car:
Breaker, Breaker, lookee here at mile marker 59,
go ahead, Lady, no sense hanging back. His voice
like the voice of God coming out of the speakers:
Today I'm not giving points for humble.

We've Been Fighting

I know enough to believe
we are lucky, you and I,
though we have spoken again today in that
angry mode (think concrete and broken glass).
I thought my job was to be efficient but
now I see my work more clearly:
to slice an orange, set each half
onto its nail, and press down, impale it
on the feeder. If I am watching when
the birds come in to land, if I see them
sip the fruit, if I call you to come look,
this is my work.
If I do not see their wings furl
and fold like fans,
see the way they face one another,
their half-oranges between them,
if I only imagine their notes
(think small conversations),
this, too, is my work. My real work.

All Night What You Said and Didn't Say

What you said and didn't say
hangs below the ceiling:
wings of a giant moth.

You rest easy,
your sleep loud
in the velvet of the hours.

I prowl the house. I'm OK.
If I've learned anything, it hasn't
shown up yet.

Under my hide,
the veins tunnel in their quiet way.
The dog is one big sigh beside me.

All night the surface of the river,
smooth and moon-silver,
covers the snags below.

It Begins with Rain

Rain turns to ice,
coating the leaves of the oak,
making the limbs sag.
You go out to stand under the tree,
shake branches, but the burden
won't shake off. You come back
for scissors, go to the oak
as you might to a grandfather,
snip, litter the ground
with iced leaves. Several limbs
do rise a bit. Oh, the second chances
you'd give me, if I'd ask.
I, who have strayed from
how I want to be. Tonight the trunk
must bear the weight, each branch
must hold. When the wind rises,
when it moves like a trickster,
the tree must stand as it has done
long days in heat or storm.
You come now into the kitchen,
your hands red with cold,
shards of ice in your hair.

The Lake in the Dark with the Geese and the Star

But the dark embraces everything:
shapes and shadows, creatures and me.
                                        —Rainer Maria Rilke

If the dark embraces everything,
it embraces us,
having come to the lake to see
the conjunction of Jupiter and Saturn.
It embraces us, standing in our parkas,
my mittens stuffed into my pocket like
an old argument.
Half-moon overhead: odd white button.
A family is beyond us down the shore,
the dad talking about their telescope,
the mom telling the kids to stop running.
The dark embraces the geese, unseen,
noisy on their sandbar, talking talking talking,
sheltered from what hunts them, and
the dark embraces also the silent paw,
the teeth of the coyote.
Saturn and Jupiter make one star
for an hour only,
something new out of being close.
The time is now, your beard
a small shine in moonlight.
I reach for your hand
because I believe in the two.
And in each one, solitary.

We Climb a Hill

The two of us sit on a hill to look out
on Branched Oak Lake,

watch a fast boat on the water below
but we hear no noise, because of

distance. Distance is what we have
when we look over the trees

and down to the water.
Distance, that thing

of ego and discussion. The two of us
at the top of a garden, as good as

the promised land, and closer. Close as your thigh
in blue denim beside me, my palm on it.

One body beside another on a perch,
we face forward

in a place we know is temporary,
and for a long bright time, leave off striving.

It Was a Four Fox Day

First, on my sunrise walk I saw her
run across Eastridge Drive
and into a yard. She scaled
the chain link fence and sat
to watch me. Her kit came out,
romped, fat and round and orange-ish,
while she stared at the two-legged.
I stared back, fascinated.
At noon and again at 4:00 I saw her
cross Mulder. Must be hunting I thought,
needs a rabbit to feed the child. At dusk
I took my puppy out on a leash. The puppy
didn't see her, kept sniffing stones, never
looked up, but I felt—the nape of my neck
felt something. I turned, and
her eyes were dark holes in her face.
They are bottomless, they are not dog eyes
or even deer eyes. It was the way she sat,
front paws together, it was her ears, large
triangles, it was her color against the shrubs,
it was how she embodied *vixen*,
the brush of her tail, turning,
it was how she floated, didn't quite
touch the grass, it was what I want, it was
belonging, it was all the time in the world.

This Is What Life Does

It gives a hotdog & paddleboat childhood,
if you're lucky, and I hope you were.
Mine was barefoot, it had bicycles
and swimming, it had some
dogma but I shucked that off.
This is what life does. For instance,
I stepped out my door before sunrise—
some people are morning people,
some--my neighbors--sleep
long sweet sleep--

and this morning
a firefly was caught in the grass
a few feet from where I stood.
I couldn't see the insect, but assumed
it by the light given off.
It couldn't get airborne, apparently,
to make those arcs in the air,
those sweeps of light their kind
are known for. This one was stuck
low in the grass,
blinked on the ground,

would have done so whether I
watched or wasn't there.
The shapes of trees made an opening,
a window for stars,
and suddenly it was as if something
important had shifted in a dream,
something useful and helpful to me.
I had been angry and felt
disrespected again, shut down, stifled,
but I mean it when I say I'm lucky.
It's what life does, gives another daybreak,
fleeting reminders, small impermanent
flashes in the grass.

Love Poem as Migraine

That morning when suddenly
I couldn't see the words in
the center of the newsfeed,
couldn't see the face in the photo,
and the twinkling space
in my vision grew larger, a sink hole
eating more and more of what was in front of me,
I thought how I'd have to change my life, blind,
have to go to the listen button,
or have you do it,
press listen and I would have to miss out
because you would not have the patience.
Later, eventually, I could see
Everything came back.
Here's what I think
about why our duet might work:
while I was visiting blindness,
trying to swallow what that would mean,
you went room to room in your practical
pajamas, picking up what I might stumble over,
and you put your coat on, put the leash on the dog,
and took him out, right on time.

I Want to Draw You in Charcoal

The light goes down in the cabin
and time is short, after
meat and beans and onions and cilantro,
after you folded your tortilla, the first one,
so the juices would have a pocket to stay in.
On the second, you said you'd use the finger-valve
method, your pinky on one side of the tortilla,
ring finger on the other, keeping the sweet
heat in. Now you're reading, but will
close the book soon, stretch and rise, walk away.
The line of the lip draws itself
when I set the edge of the charcoal on the paper
at the place where your warm breath reaches.
Now brow and nose, the shadow under your chin.
The light is dimming. The bats
no doubt flicker from pine to pine,
making a living. I draw the arm
but you shift--
I rub it out, pick up the black smudge
with a little square of chamois.
Now you hold the book above your face.
But I cannot get it right
before you change again. You turn in the couch
and everything is different. One knee up,
one down, now you're on your side. I go with
the arm as I have begun it, imagine how it would
hold the book if it held the book as it used to,
fake it, looking at what is real before me,
drawing what I want to see.

The Reason

Because there was that week in Europe
when I wore the green shirt or the blue-striped
and we rode the trains.

Because there was that day on the Ute trail
when the wind was bad and we had to
keep a hand-hold always on the rocks.
We could see the elk herd
like dots in the canyon below.

Because there was that morning we hid in the trees
to watch the cranes on the sandbars in the river,
waiting for the roar of the flock when they rose.
The roar lifted us, we said, out of our boots.

Because there was that night
we walked along the ocean with our dog,
a wave running up to lick our feet,
another wave, another.
My life, your life,
our hands close to one another,
sometimes touching.

Horses, Free

Open the doors of the barns
and follow the horses out into the world,
follow the hollow tapping of their hooves,
and see the streets their great hearts find
to amble in, and which gate they will
come back to, like me,
for food and touch.

I choose the building, house, tent,
where you and I stand together,
the enclosure where we face,
or turn our backs,
where we give small things,
some tangible,
one to the other.

Declutter

Yellow rug, pitch it. Dented kettle, pitch it.
One leather mitten from Scotland,
the other gone for years, left
on a bus or dropped in the parking lot
of the Ordway. Do not throw out
Ordway. Save Scotland. Save
mornings, the books, a pot of tea. Save
the slant of sun on the floor.
Save the chairs, the varnish of one
spotted because of my long hair
dripping at breakfast. Save the kitchen,
save the meals we had there, the first one,
my place at the table, the place
which was mine ever after,
save the small box beside my plate,
save the opals you gave,
a blossom for each ear.
You went to get two pears
from a stash in the basement,
down the stairs to fetch them, save the pears,
save the best one, the prince of pears,
save it into your palm. The lines of it,
the intersection of your line and mine.
The cut the hope the promise the need,
time never long enough, save the stubborn
thin-skinned fullness of it, save the delicious
length of you, throw out my fear,
save the everlasting feast.

Looking for Meteors

We have the time wrong for the meteor shower,
but we don't know that, you and I on the dam,
looking up into the cosmos, my neck

bent like a piece of cardboard.
We jump and point
at a couple of false alarms,

airplanes and a possible satellite.
We lie down, wrapped deep into
the jacket we share, not searching anymore.

Arcturus hangs like a pearl within reach
in her appointed place on the throat of the west.
There's Polaris, so shy, though everything

does turn under her arm. Antares has
become a homefire burning. Cassiopeia
is now arms and legs of lovers:

tangled, cocooned, bound
in their own unstreaked coat.

I Dreamed I Was in Ireland, Love

I don't know where you were.
I went walking on one green hillside
after another with two sweet little
schoolgirls, lasses, you might say.
There was a picnic table under
no ceiling but sky. Where were you,
Love, I wonder, while I was feasting
in the company of children?
Remember that time we got married,
that was real, wasn't it, in the snow
on Mount Evans? We tramped in
drifts up to our knees, laughing, stumbling.
I wore that blue ski jacket you bought me
before the time of any harsh words.
We paused in a cathedral of snow,
tall pines for rafters, and said our vows.
Couldn't be found now,
made as it was of vapor and flake
and ancient words like *cherish* and *thee*.
And then later in the dream,
I left the borrowed house again
and tried to re-find the place,
the picnic. You know that
kind of dream, Love, where you are
searching, but the prize is
always still out there somewhere.
So the moral of the story is perhaps:
go hand in hand beside the one
whose face you need across the table
when you look over the rim
of the fine China, or paper, cup.
The one you desire, reachable,
as we might be--I'll try for it--
arm's length and getting closer,
in this strange and misty land
where we find ourselves, could
really find ourselves, today.

IV.

Homemade Soup and Rolls and Conversation

Homemade Soup and Rolls and Conversation

It's been good, this dinner party, but
suddenly I'm misunderstood, so I

try to put a patch on it, like those patches
on the inner tubes we floated

down the Keya Paha when we were
kids, the summers long and open,

sand bars to run on and rest on. I try to
explain away my blunder

but the inner tube springs another leak,
air hissing out a little hole, making bubbles.

I can swim, I'm not going to drown, but there goes
my easy float on the current. The topic of discussion

is going to change fast. I have one sentence to
insert here, if I'm lucky, to keep my head above water.

What to Talk About

After you cut off the head of the chicken,
hold the feet, and dunk the body
up and down in a pail of scalding water;

pull or rub the sodden hot feathers off,
then with a very sharp blade, cut up
the carcass, and discard the innards.

Do it again. Repeat. Chill the meat
in ice water in a big enamel pan (only
cool spot in the sweltering kitchen).

All that chicken:
thighs, breasts, legs, necks, wings, backs.
Pack the pieces into plastic bags, layer them

into the freezer, close the lid,
be done done done. You'd
think this training would be good for

something. Maybe how to make Word quit
capitalizing every line, or how to keep track
of what you changed the password to

for some account or other. I doubt it.
Wet feathers to get rid of,
mounds of pink and gray guts, bury them

in a new hole in the pasture or the gully.
Turn away, run away to college, to
the biggest town in the county, the state.

Keep running from the smell of
feathers. Don't talk of it. Don't talk.
Maybe tell about shaping the rim

of a pie crust. That's pretty. Tell
about peeling the red apples, buckets of
apples. Don't talk about the chickens.

Today I Got Lost and It Was Good

Today on the trail down Madera Canyon
I got lost because I went wrong
at one of the switchbacks. It looked like a trail
for a while. When it thinned out, disappeared
into the ether, or the earth, I tried to
find my way back. Lost, though
every scrub pine, every dead mesquite
held out a least one arm for me,
while every boulder turned its back.
The sticker bushes were extroverts
and they hurt. I had my walkie-talkie
in hand and it worked, hallelujah, so I
radioed my friends who were already at the
meet-up point, each waiting with sack lunch
and good sense of direction--I told them I'd
go on down the gorge I now
found myself in; it'll probably come out
at the road, I told them, and myself,
several times. Actually the gorge finally
came out on the back side of the Santa Rita Lodge.
The only thing between me and civilization was
then a fence, near which stood a sizeable granite
chunk, a relative of the granite and schist and aggregate
which had been my good friends all down the gorge,
except when they tossed me into the brambles.
I crawled—scraped, actually—up onto this last
granite near the fence, and made it over,
and made it over the unhelpful remark
from one of my reunited party, the remark
I tried to like but couldn't, quite.
Maybe if I live a long time, which I am
going to start doing right now,
I'll gain from today:
how I stayed happy—that's the wrong word but
it's the word I'll use, because when I get flustered
I lose. I lose altitude, I lose the path, I lose it all. Oh I

admit to stupidity, yes, that's easy. Also to not
paying attention. Maybe it's the same thing.
Someday I will know how to stay
in the center of being alive and human and wrong
and right. And today I liked how close I came.

I Give Myself Advice

Make yourself step out of the cave,
the thoughts you have become
used to, the bad stuff you've been

breathing as if it nourished, fed your
bones--but how can I live with what
happened? If you can make your legs

work for one step into the yard,
maybe the sun is there,
lighting the grass like green neon,

the new little whippersnapper tree
stands upright in the place where you
had the old tree sawed off and dug out.

Chances are the sky will show up
in pieces behind the row of pines.
The new maple, spindly thing,

you could pretend it is
the friend you wronged—or did she
wrong you?--her eyes

asking, after all these eons,
will you lift one heavy arm
and wave?

Just When You'd Begun to Feel

you had nailed it, the summer's
daily red cardinal clicking in the shrubs,
heat and cicadas in the high oak,
lawn chair and lemonade,
the glass wet in your hand,
there comes a day when
a cool gust out of nowhere
whirlwinds a bunch of yellow leaves
onto the grass. It is what your
mother said: We grow too soon old
and too late smart. You need to find
a sweater in the mishmash. You need
more funds, more friends, more courage.
This is about winter: the north wind
behind that teasing breeze. The way
those yellow leaves spiral
to the ground—that's you.
Ambition has been holding you aloft
in insubstantial air and then,
with a pretty flick of the wrist,
dances you down, down.

I Brought You Here, Beautiful Daughter

This world, I don't know
how to explain it to you.
Snarling dog, powerful jaw,
paws to push you off balance,
teeth for your soft throat. Daily
news which tears your heart.
And yet there is
also the young bony gray
cat which trots toward you
when you walk by, wanting
only to rub against
your ankle. Go ahead, child,
pat the head and ears of the world
that offers such contrast. I would
give you goodness, if I could. If I
could, myself, be free of the other.

The Day You Were Born

Rain was turning to snow, and my father, nervous,
drove through the dark, the windshield wipers

whispering over and over. I groaned,
holding my hands to my belly

for sixty miles, and counting. You were ready
in the way of new things. The world

may be decided by opening, by change.
Well, I was young, too,

and we both thrived. Look how every season
your hair is more wonderful in its

fall down your back, its orderly cascade,
your swan fingers through it,

how you move it in a gentle way,
like everything, into place. What I learn

from you! Let me know this:
an honor to call you, wait for your voice,

madcap woman, running before the mortal wind,
saying: Hi Mom, what's up?

Getting the Room Ready

You'd think I was preparing
for his birth, the way I polish

surfaces with a damp cloth, arrange
the photos. He'll be looking at what

I place carefully on the clean shelves.
He may open a book, focus on a face

or mountain. He'll be here only the one night,
then roll on to his meetings, his work,

because life, I've noticed, is a freight train,
determined and brief,

but I purge the space for him,
carry away to the basement

what doesn't belong, doesn't
serve, and leave for his beloved eye

that which will interest or matter
as he does. He does.

It Seems There Are Talkers

and not-talkers. My father
was a not-talker. He didn't
need to. The roofers, crew of
two, strangers in town--they
were the talkers. Talked all the time
about anything. I was captivated.
Dad smiled, quiet. They talked me
into letting them give Skipper,
our white Spitz, a haircut.
The shorn dog
stood in the fallen tufts,
wondering what happened—
that's me today. My sort-of
friend is yammering on,
showing me up for stupid,
as I stand, wordless,
on the spot she always puts me on,
noticing with my one good eye
the flashing of the scissors
in her hand. Watch out.
She's not done yet.

Looking for Approval in All the Wrong Places

I got accustomed to adoration
a long time ago. My mother fed it to me
from a dixie cup and I got to liking, licking it

daily. There's no easy way out of it now.
I want my friends to approve and affirm
any idea of mine that rolls out of the hangar

at our weekly get-together. I want to
gobsmack the entire room with my wit.
Is that too much to ask?

It's too much to ask, isn't it? Their eyes
all interest while I expound. I've been
steering my ego down this

concrete highway, so
sure of how to be.
headlights on, this road trip,

mile after mile, faster, faster.
What I'm looking for slides by in the dark

again and again, the bright flash of a yardlight
showing up and then, just as quick, gone.

Come with Me to the Land of Brag

This is the method: drop big names
to get where you're trying to go.
What I said to the famous man
is a nice flat stone for the right foot,
what he said to me is another flat stone
for the left foot, and so on to make the ascent,
but at the top of the hill
there is another brag to climb, which climb my
father in his honesty didn't do. I shouldn't
have believed what the world said when it said
it's who you know. I see us working
to repair some machine, me in my thin jacket,
my father in his gray sweatshirt, the hood up to
keep the nape of his neck from the Dakota wind.
There, he says, one last tap on the
carburetor, Let's see if this damn thing
will run today. Except he hardly ever said damn,
unless it was of more importance than carburetors.
Sometimes still I hear him clear his throat and
get back to work. He is a window I'm looking through
into the house I am, one room of it: two flowered
couches at an angle good for conversation,
a dish of peanuts on the coffee table,
and a ceramic cardinal, its crest
trying to be as red as the real bird
I saw on the grass a fleeting moment ago.

He Fell Through the Ice

The story says the child survived,
ran from the pond to the farmhouse

after falling in, the ice too
mysterious to hold him, as the story
barely holds him now. A strong hand

pulled him out, water streaming
from his coat and boots and mittens,
one of the uncles having hooked him

by the collar and brought him up to
daylight in the way rescue happens
after cold reality enters into the ears,
fills the mouth, takes the breath.

This much is known: the child stood
shivering on the bank, and his father,
in the heavy layers required of the work,

came, knelt in front of him—thankful—
I think I can add thankful to the story—
knelt, looked into his eyes, said his name,

straightened perhaps the soggy collar,
and said: "Run home, boy,
don't stop. If you stop, you'll die."
The words have come down

from that hour, intact. The men went
back to their work, cutting blocks of ice
and loading them, and the boy did run

across the pasture--he's running toward me now
through the years, his feet in his boots
pounding the frozen ground,

doing what must be done,
this child, my father. He ducks under
or clambers over at least one fence,

sees home ahead of him. The house,
the chimney, the clapboard and windows
come into sight, and the door with its scars.

He bursts red-cheeked into the kitchen.
His mother turns,

as a mother often does, from baking or
washing or chopping or mending, and
there is her child standing squarely

in the story. Now she is peeling off his shirt,
toweling him dry, his skin cool to her touch,
but warming.

Thinking of Her as the Leaves Fall

The backyard maple lets go
of what it has kept at the end of each twig.
I've blamed her and been ashamed.

The blouse she sewed—
I wouldn't wear it—didn't sass but left it
on the hanger for years just as she'd

buttoned it there. I was her sounding board
when she railed against my father
and I couldn't agree with that.

Still don't, but now I see
how she grew into the shape she'd been
bent. Don't I?

Today let me send out roots
into the dark, seeking what I need.
I stand, arms raised,

where I've been planted.
In rain or sun or soft white fog.

She gave me what she could,
and I pass it on.

Why is This the Plan?

She, who had worked so hard,
chanted *Keep-a-going, keep-a-going*
after she lost her mind. Body

sturdy and thick, but what she
said and did too loony and
frightening. There was no talking

her out of an idea; there was no
reasoning when she escaped to
the sidewalks at night. She didn't

need sleep, her jaw set and the kitchen
drawers full of knives. Is this what we
come to? Our children putting us away

in locked wards, people paid to
herd us? Couldn't you provide
green pastures and streams for us to

lie down in, like old bovines,
chewing and staring? You promised
soft grass, birds singing.

She Had No Better Guide

than the round white dollop of moon,
not the same tonight as last night,
waning, hiding out in the galaxy

or showing just a fingernail.
No constant, that deceiver. Now
she's taken her light, what there

was of it, behind the mountain.
I pack for the journey: shoes I can
jam on quickly, my expired
license, thin layers of folding money
from the drawer, my coat of many colors,

the lie I've been considering,
the bravado, if I can find where
I stashed it. You have a good head
on your shoulders, she said that time
she put me on the bus to California
with only a twenty-dollar bill. Use it.

I Get on the Pony of My Imagination

I gallop around in my hometown,
up and down the gravel streets. What
a satisfying sound the hooves

of the Shetland make. I've just
attended confirmation class at
a clapboard church where the pastor

corrected me mightily: No, the earth is
not millions of years old, it's only
6000 X 365 and some odd

days since God created it for Adam.
So now I know, and am free to ride
to the east end of town, tie the pony

at the gate of Mae Klein's house,
go to her screen door and politely ask for
her sugar cookie recipe, my mother having

called ahead to arrange. And Mae Klein,
with her fountain pen, having written how much
flour, how much butter, one sheet of paper,

blue ink complete with flourishes, I'm mounted
to ride, but oh Lordy this black and white hellion
takes the bit in her teeth and heads for the board fence

at the Brockemier place, yes, she's going to scrape me
off. She trots, her smooth hide sliding along the boards,
I have to raise my leg to keep from getting it crushed,

I'm losing my balance. That's what this is: rejection
letters from editors, the prestigious journal has
turned me down again, thank you for sending, you

dreamer, you. I'm dumped unceremoniously. The pony
runs, triumphant, reins flopping like ribbons in the wind.

Girl Playing the Violin

A teenager plays her violin
on the dock as people line up
to get on their buses for
tours of Nova Scotia. She is
Nova Scotia for me, or maybe
the whole continent, her long
legs in their black jeans and boots,
her lean arms which seem
to love her violin.
The angle of her cheek
against the instrument,
the music up and
out from near her heart
toward the raw-boned sky.
The man in line behind me
says this is exploitation of a minor,
which statement makes him perhaps
feel better about not tipping and
which makes me take some bills
in my hand, my hand which cannot
bow and glide, cannot rise and move
bird-like over the strings.
I step out of line
and walk to the violin case
open on the ground, drop
my bills in, an excuse
to get close to the face of music.
The sound of my heels as I walk,
my breath in the bellows of my ribs,
a proof I want to learn, if I can,
how to smile with my eyes,
keep playing, nod a very small nod
while staying in the exact center of the note,
because the thing is music,
music is the only thing.

You Need a Secretary

to keep track of everything, the repair
to the ceiling, the trip to Missouri and

it's your turn to have people over for
pizza, there's the writing group you

need to attend and connect with
and did you really cancel Reese Construction

or will they show up Monday at 9:30 and
your spouse will go ballistic What now--

dizziness--is it stress or is it cancer. It's
overload and you must do this,

keep all the balls in the air. Air,
that's what you need. Air, and a secretary.

I Had to Cancel Fun Stuff for Friday

because Friday I'll be dealing
with a ton of other stuff. This
paradise is more like a Throw-

Her-to-the-Lions act and I am not
the one with claws. My backpack
is chock-full of musts and shoulds

and other iron ingots.
I'm ahead at the moment and
that's good, but soon enough,

soon enough, I feel the hot breath
of the one who's hell-bent on
catching me, running as I am

in my stocking feet, feeling every
pebble in the arena, because last week

when I was feeling so happy, I
tossed my shoes away.

The Dancing Queen in the Grocery Store

My husband and I stop in at Hy-Vee
to pick up milk and soup

and because I'm looking at all this abundance
and know much from every store
can end up in the landfill—

and because a song is
beginning to play in the speakers—
who chooses these things?--

and because it's ABBA, and because
I feel the beat of the tambourine, oh yeah
I can dance, I can jive

I'm not really dancing—do you think I'm crazy?—
but I feel like I'm dancing

because my knees are feeling dancerly
and because I'm wearing a pair of old boots
which have danced many miles

and because we begin to add this and that to our cart
(I pick up a box of crackers which I need
and a jar of Tahini Premium Sesame Paste, which I don't)

and because Noah at the cash register, young, with glasses,
last week suspected
I was trying to get away with a bag of cherries,
and will, I know, send me off with
a phrase about the rest of my day,

and because my husband is now choosing between
Hearty Beef Barley and Chunky Pub-Style Chicken Pot Pie—
who names these things?

and because I don't have to choose—
I can have it all, I can dance, I can jive—
I go right on having the time of my life.

What I've Heard About Jane Austen

Jane leaned over her papers at a small desk
in a room on the second floor
and when for some reason—company came,
or someone cried or bled into their handkerchief,

the maid was pouty, or her father sniffed--
then Jane folded up what she was writing
and did what must be done. Soon she
came back to the dance or the argument

or the decision her character must make
on the page. Jane picked up the pen and
dipped into the ink, the dance went on or
someone won the argument. That's what I

need to learn, Jane long dead, Jane dust and grit
in your coffin. Before I take my place on
the satin of mine—oh wait—I'm going to
be cremated—before I hide in my powdery

ashes with bits of my tooth enamel,
I want to learn to deal with distractions,
or quit manufacturing them,
decide how I'm going to be today,

just today, rise from where I'm stuck
and float with good will toward
what it is I have to do.

We Step into Tina's

that hole in the wall
cafe on South Street for 30 years.
We step in at some early hour
when the cinnamon rolls are
just out of the oven, the pan still
in fact in Tina's hand, the hand with
the red mitt potholder,
the hand that has started from
scratch again this morning.
We take our usual booth and Tina
comes over with the coffee pot,
sets down a white cup for you
and a white cup for me. She's not
really Tina—it's Tina's daughter
what's-her-name--
the deal goes on and on
as you and I want to
forever, but we've been drifting,
fighting, and you don't care
what I'm wanting and I don't
tell you. What is to become of us?
Tina, or her stand-in for the real thing,
has filled your cup and mine. She
looks up and asks: "The usual?"
Now one of us, or both of us,
must answer.

What To Do Now?

My friend Teri says her first memory
is fear, because her father
got a kick out of scaring her by
dangling a rubber frog near her face
while she cried and her
mother begged the man to stop.
How could a father enjoy that? My own
first memory is sitting alone
on the back step of a house, I'm
eating a radish, I have a little bowl
of soft butter to dip the radish in.
The butter is good,
the radish hot but not
burning, and I'm hearing sounds
in the tall pines near the fence.
I try to--but can't--see what is there--
it was crows hidden in foliage—
no danger, just mystery.
It's the luck of the draw and Teri got
a bum deal. What to do now? Eat
butter or its alcoholic equivalent,
do some good today if
the opportunity shows up, kiss
the face that appears in my kitchen
at dinner, twirl the body I'm
living in, and keep listening for those crows.

Memorized Eight Lines

What are those blue remembered hills?
—A.E. Housman (1859-1936)

I can recite Housman's lines
about blue remembered hills
that cannot come again.
I have no blue remembered hills—
mine was an expanse of prairie grass—
but I have losses which are deep
and burn and trouble me. Don't you?
I am my own mixture, my
history, my jealousies, how
I did not—do not—promote a friend's
best interests. I lack the generosity.
Yet when the poem touches the harp
within my ribs, my unique array of cells,
when it strums my sorrow with its nimble
hand, when its thumb and fingers pluck
the strings, though they have different names,
the throbbing shakes this body that is me
with the song I did not write.

Rhoda Writes About the Corn

She sharpened her pencil with a paring knife,
my ancestor Rhoda Miranda Sanders Moses,

and sat at the oilcloth of the table on her farm
to write to her grown son

asking if he could send money,
or the bank would foreclose on her little place.

She loved her cornfield: the rows
standing at attention as she came by

on her way to the post office. She almost didn't
write about the silk, the nubbins in the ear,

tassel after tassel reaching into summer heat,
the rustle of corn growing

She decided to add the post script because
there was room at the bottom of the page,

and because there was time
as she sat in her buckboard

on main street before going in to mail it.
She took from her handbag the stubby pencil

and she nosed its point along
with a faint scratching noise—

what a thing writing is—
she put what she saw and felt

onto the paper, folded and
creased it with her withered hand,
and it comes, unfolding, down to me.

It's Odd to Use These Symbols

Shapes, scratches, signs,
this alphabet we've been taught--
I can reach into myself,
whatever my self is, and pull
out ideas with this code,
this language, these indicators
on a screen. I can examine,
using curls and lines, my thoughts.
We are, as my father used to say
fearfully and wonderfully made, and even
that string of words is here because symbols
were pressed into clay or drawn on
animal skin in some language I
don't know, on a hillside I've only
read about. Thank you, language,
and those who hunched over a
surface to write, taking time from being
in the real world, whatever that is, to
inscribe, as I am doing, setting down
marks I can use,
as grains of sand may be
stood upon to look up or out.
A fast truck came by in the dark
again tonight, and I was saved because it
stayed on the road while I stayed on the beach,
a good arrangement. The full moon was
exactly overhead, exactly in the
center of a halo of white. Vapor, is it?
Illumination and trickery? I didn't
stay for long, I was there in my
brown boots and black coat,
the moon was an iris,
and I write to
keep the ring around it,
as I keep my father,
who may be gone forever.
Except in language. His clear
unblinking eye, the will to work.
Let me applaud words which
keep what would slip away.

Golden

We were on vacation, our car needed repair,
the mechanic said it would be done when

it was done. So we walked where
our feet led. The light was

golden on us. You and I, the table, the cups.
We talked. We had these words in our mouths:

oak, cask, cork, body, bouquet. Side by side
we found streets we did not foresee.

You said the soft rain melted
before it touched the ground.

Slow the race. Once in a while there's a gift,
these brief hours we wander together.

Acknowledgments

She Went to the Fair	*The Fourth River*
This Is Her Territory, Not Mine	*The Fourth River*
I Don't Know Which River I Am	*The Fourth River*
Will You Write About the Painted Ladies?	*I-70 Review*
Dancing on My Mother's Rug	*Platte Valley Review*
What Work Was	*Poetry of Presence II*
Horses, Galloping	*Prairie Schooner*
This is What Life Does	*Rattle*
It's Odd to Use These Symbols	*bosque*
How'd She Win the Heart of That Guy?	*Midwest Quarterly*
Today I Got Lost and It Was Good	*Midwest Quarterly*
Why Is This the Plan?	*MockingHeart Review*

About the Author

FAST HORSE is Marjorie Saiser's ninth book of poems. Saiser writes of our relationships and everyday life, as well as our connection to the natural world. She has co-edited an anthology of poems and prose written by women on the Great Plains, and her work has been published in *Prairie Schooner, American Life in Poetry, Nimrod, Rattle, RHINO, Chattahoochee Review, Poetry East, Poet Lore,* and other journals. She earned a Master's Degree in Creative Writing at UN-L. Recognition for her poetry includes the High Plains Book Award, the Willa Award, Leo Love Award, Little Blue Stem Award, and finalist for the Robert Penn Warren Prize.

www.ingramcontent.com/pod-product-compliance
Lightning Source LLC
Chambersburg PA
CBHW020213090426
42734CB00008B/1046